Birds of
Devon Hedg

Sandra Chalton

Orchard Publications

Published by Orchard Publications

Orchard is an imprint of Tor Mark,

United Downs Ind Est, Redruth, Cornwall TR16 5HY

First Published 2006; this edition 2016

ISBN 978 1 898964 68 1

Redwing – a winter-visiting thrush

Printed by Hedgerow Print Ltd, Marsh Lane,
Lords Meadow, Crediton EX17 1ES

INTRODUCTION

A small bird's life is fraught with danger, whether from predators, extremes of weather (especially hard winters) or shortage of food. Survival rates of fledglings are low.

The birds I have illustrated depend on healthy hedgerows with both dense shrubbery and some uncut trees, as well as plenty of wildflowers beneath to attract insects and to produce seeds. Their diet, consisting of insects - at all stages (egg, pupa, larva and adult), seeds and fruits, means that the use of pesticides and herbicides endangers their survival. Where farmland has mature hedgerows, some laid and cut to produce dense foliage, some uncut or cut only every three years and in rotation to allow fruiting; with a few standard trees such as oak and ash, and in addition wide wild field margins, we maximise the chances of a healthy population of small birds. Ideally the hedges shouldn't be cut before late autumn, as some finches in particular often nest late to ensure availability of seeds for their fledglings.

The best time to see and hear birds in general is early spring, when males are establishing their territories and finding a mate, usually singing enthusiastically from exposed perches. Of course, in a garden, the birdfeeder will attract many birds needing to supplement their diet in winter. July to August most birds are moulting and keep a low profile in thick foliage. In autumn the abundant fruits and seeds will attract them and many will be seen in flocks.

I have painted adult male and sometimes female birds. When the female is less colourful than the male I comment on it in the description. Young birds lack the full colour plumage of adults and so are more difficult to identify.

When writing about the birds I have included phonetic descriptions of their songs and calls (though these can differ from book to book and it is very difficult to produce phonetically the sounds that birds make). It is of course best if you can actually see them singing.

Fieldfare – a winter-visiting thrush

WARBLERS

These are the birds I find most difficult to recognise, as do many other people, hence the expression 'little, brown bird', which is often used to refer to them.

They have thin, straight, pointed bills and can be glimpsed restlessly flitting in and out of the undergrowth, searching for insects - the major part of their diet. They also nest in dense vegetation, low down in hedges. Most are migratory, arriving in spring and leaving again in autumn.

They are probably best known for their distinctive warbling songs, by which the different species can be recognised.

WILLOW WARBLER

One of the smaller warblers at 4½ inches (11cm) in length, it is olive green to pale brown, with pale undersides. Its song is a musical, liquid, soft, descending warble; its call a plaintive 'fooeed'.

It is a migrant bird, wintering in Africa, usually arriving here about the first week in April. It hunts restlessly and with much wing-flicking, for insects, particularly in newly opened pussy-willow catkins and other blossoms.

The males generally arrive first, define their territory and, on the arrival of the females, pair up and start breeding. The nest is of twigs and grass and is feather-lined; it is domed, with a side opening and usually on the ground, at the foot of a hedge. The females lay about 6 eggs to a clutch, white with pinkish brown speckles. Sometimes they will manage to produce two broods before leaving in September. The willow warbler is unusual in moulting completely twice a year.

Willow warbler on pussy willow

CHIFFCHAFF

Also 4½ inches (11cm) in length and very difficult to distinguish from the willow warbler, except by its very distinctive, monotonously repeated 'chiff-chaff' usually sung from a high tree. Its call is a plaintive 'hooeed'. It is pale brown with pale undersides and usually has a darker leg colouring than the willow warbler.

It is the first warbler to arrive in spring, many over-wintering in the Mediterranean, but some staying here in the south west of England.

The ball-shaped nest is built in dense vegetation, such as nettles and brambles, near the ground. The female lays 6 or 7 white eggs with purplish-brown speckles.

Chiffchaff on elder

Blackcap

Slightly larger at 5½ inches (14cm) and easily distinguished by its 'cap': the male's is black and the female's brown. Its song is a short, mellow, musical warble of rising strength, given from a well-covered perch.

Although migrant, a few are now over-wintering in the South West. Others arrive in April to May. They are mainly insectivorous but will feed at bird tables, and in late summer will also stock up on berries. They often nest deep in a bramble patch. The nest is a cup of dried grass and roots lined with finer grass and sometimes hair, with 4 to 6 eggs laid.

Blackcap (male and female) on elder

GARDEN WARBLER

5½ inches (14cm) long with a brown upperside and greyish-white underside. It has a more rounded head than other warblers. It stays well hidden in the foliage of hedges and bramble thickets (not particularly in gardens) even while singing. Its song is musical, mellow and liquid, similar to the blackcap's but longer and more subdued. Its call is a sharp 'tak'. The nest is usually built lower down in the hedge than the black cap's and is made of grass, stems and twigs, forming a cup, lined with finer grass and hair and containing 4 to 5 eggs.

Garden warbler on bramble

Whitethroat

Also 5½ inches (14cm) in length, the male has a greyish hood, the female's is brown, both have light brown wings, a white throat, and a longish tail with white outer edges. It is very active, moving through bushes and shrubbery, searching for insects. Its song, given in flight or from a covered perch, is a fast, short, high-pitched warble. It sings later into summer than other warblers. The call is a rasping 'tze'.

It is a summer visitor from Central Africa, often nesting amongst stinging nettles. The male builds several nests, only one of which will be used, with grasses and roots forming a cup, lined with hair. There are usually two clutches laid, each of 4 or 5 eggs.

Whitethroat (male and female) on hawthorn

GOLDCREST

At a length of 3½ inches (9cm) it is our smallest bird, easily recognised by its black-edged 'gold' crest - the female's is yellow, the male's more orange, particularly displayed during courtship. It has greenish upper parts, paler underneath.

Although it is usually found high up in coniferous and mixed woods, outside the breeding season it can be seen in hedges and shrubs. Its tiny sharp beak is ideally suited to winkling out the minuscule insects in conifer foliage and the places where other birds can't reach.

Its call is thin and high-pitched; the song is similar, ending in a short warble. The nest is finely woven with moss, lichen and cobwebs, and is suspended under a branch - usually of a conifer. There are 7 to 10 eggs, white to buff with purple or brown speckles.

Goldcrest (male and female) on ivy

THRUSHES

This is a large family which in fact includes some smaller birds: wheatears, redstarts, and the robin amongst others. All have well-developed songs, long legs and upright, alert stances on the ground.

SMALLER THRUSHES (CHATS)

ROBIN

A very familiar sight, particularly in winter, with its bright orange/red face and breast, with a pale grey border, brown upperparts and pale underparts, (young birds are speckled brown all over). It is often seen on or near the ground and is given to bowing and tail-flicking, drooping its wings and hopping rapidly on its long, thin legs. It is 5 inches (13cm) long and has a sharp beak, feeding primarily on insects and worms. In this country it has become quite tame and will follow gardeners around waiting for the soil to be turned over to expose 'treats'. It will also eat seeds and fruit in season and is often found in hedgerows. It will sometimes 'hover' in front of the hedge.

Its song is a series of high-pitched, fast, warbling notes, building up in volume and usually delivered from a low perch. The alarm call is a thin, sharp 'tsiiih' and, when nervous, it gives an accelerating 'tic-tic-tic...'. It has large eyes and good night vision and will often sing at night by street lights (even feeding on flying insects there). Along with the blackbird, it is one of the first singers in the dawn chorus, and will also sing all year round (except when moulting in late summer). The male defends its territory aggressively from other males.

The female builds the nest, usually in ivy on walls or trees or in undergrowth on banks, and sometimes in sheds in old containers. The nest is made of grass, dead leaves and moss lined with fine roots and hair. There may be two clutches a year of 5 or 6 eggs.

Robin on holly

TRUE THRUSHES

Medium-sized birds with slender bills and long wings and tails. Most have spotted undersides, juveniles are always spotted. They feed on worms, invertebrates and fruit and can often be seen standing or running on open ground. Outside the breeding season they can be seen in loose flocks.

They build open cup-shaped nests in trees or bushes with a clutch of 3 to 6 eggs.

BLACKBIRD

10 inches (25cm) long, the male is black with a bright yellow bill and narrow yellow eye-ring; the female all brown with mottled underparts. Its song is a musical fluting warble; the warning call is a repeated 'pink-pink-pink'. It sings from an open perch, particularly at dusk and dawn - often the first voice in the dawn chorus!

Blackbirds forage for worms on open grass but also eat insects and, in the late summer and winter, gorge themselves on berries and fruit of all kinds. They nest early and often manage two broods, with 3 to 5 pale blue/green speckled eggs per clutch. The nest is a cup of dried grass, twigs, rootlets and moss, lined with mud and dried grass, in a hedge or low tree.

Blackbird (male) on rowan

SONG THRUSH

Slightly smaller than the blackbird at 9 inches (23cm) and not so common. The upper body is brown and the underparts spotted with brown on the white belly and cream-shaded breast. It has buff/yellow underwings. Its song is 'virtuoso', flute-like and very varied with short sections repeated, and often lasting five minutes or more. It can be heard almost any time of year, singing from a high perch. Although found mainly in woods, parks and gardens, it can be seen searching the undergrowth or leaf-litter under hedges for snails, which it will then smash open on a stone 'anvil'. It will also feed on insects and worms and on berries in autumn.

Breeding begins early. The female builds a nest of grass and twigs lined with mud or wood pulp. There are 4 to 6 light blue, speckled eggs.

The song thrush often doesn't survive very harsh winters and it is a partial migrant, some birds moving to lower ground for the winter or flying to Southern Europe. A decline in population of 53% over twenty-five years may be connected to the use of poisonous slug pellets in gardens, as snails are the thrush's emergency food; however there has been an upturn in numbers in the last few years.

Song thrush with snail

MISTLE THRUSH

At 11 inches (28cm) long this thrush is bigger than the song thrush. It can be distinguished from it also by its larger breast spots and more erect posture on the ground. In flight it shows white underwings and has a characteristic flapping and closing of wings. Its song is a series of short, flute-like notes delivered from the top of a tree. It will sing throughout winter, even in stormy weather, which led to its popular name of 'stormcock'. Its call, in flight, is a rattling chatter.

Although usually found in mature woods, edge of woodland or on open grassland, in autumn to winter they will be seen around large, established, fruiting hedgerows. A pair will requisition a berry-bearing tree or shrub - particularly holly - keeping all other birds off until, when their favourite food of slugs, snails, worms and insects is in short supply, they will eat the fruit. The berries often stay on their chosen tree throughout winter until a freezing spell - even as late as March. They will also defend hawthorn or yew or the first ivy berries.

The female builds the nest, usually in a high fork of a tree and lays 3 to 5 eggs, cream to turquoise with purplish brown spots. Sometimes there will be a second brood. Some birds will fly to the continent for the winter.

REDWING AND FIELDFARE

(See pages 2 & 3)

These thrushes are winter visitors from Northern Europe, travelling the countryside in large flocks, sometimes together, in search of food - grassland invertebrates or wild fruit. They can be seen in open fields and visiting larger uncut hedgerows, where they particularly favour hawthorn berries.

The redwing is easily distinguished from the song thrush by the red patches on its flanks and under its wings. It is 8 inches (20cm) in length. Its song is a short repetition of flute-like notes followed by a low warble. The call is a high-pitched 'zee-up'. The fieldfare is a larger bird - up to 10 inches (25cm) but variable. It has a grey head and rump, chestnut-brown back, dark tail and spotted underside. It has a twittering song, often given in flight; its call is a loud 'schack, schack'.

Mistle thrush

FINCHES

Small to medium-sized birds. Their bills are short and heavy, suitable for cracking open seeds. They are often brightly coloured, the male more so than the female. They are usually found in flocks outside the breeding season. They may nest in trees or shrubs, in weeds or on the ground.

GOLDFINCH

A very attractive little bird at 5 inches (12cm) in length with distinctive colouration: yellow bars on black wings, a white rump and black and white head with red on its face (slightly less on the female). Its song, given from an exposed perch, is a liquid twittering, its call a repeated 'deedelit'.

It is usually seen in a small flock, known as a 'charm'. It feeds on weed seeds, favouring thistle, but will supplement its diet with insects. It likes open land with some trees and bushes and can be seen 'dancing' along the hedgerows on foraging flights.

The female builds the nest in the upper branches of small trees or shrubs; a woven cup of plant material, including thistledown. She lays 4-6 eggs: pale bluish-white with a few reddish-brown streaks. Several breeding pairs will nest near each other. Goldfinches will often nest late - even into August, so that they can feed their nestlings on the developing 'milky' seeds of thistle.

Goldfinch on spear-thistle

GREENFINCH

Bigger and stockier than the goldfinch at 5½ inches (14cm) the male is an overall olive-green with distinctive yellow flashes on the tail and wings; the female is browner. It has a large pinkish beak with which it breaks open seeds. It forages over a wide area, often in flocks; pairs will also nest near to each other.

It has a pleasant, rapid, twittering song, finishing off with 4 or 5 musical notes: 'tew, tew, tew, tew' and a final 'greeee'. Its call is a quiet 'chi, chi, chi, chi'. It usually sings from a bush or tree top or during a display flight.

The nest is cup-shaped, formed with twigs, stems and moss and lined with hair, fine stems and sometimes a few feathers. 4-6 eggs are laid, greyish-white to pale greenish-blue, with a sparse speckling of reddish-brown, black or lilac. There may be two or three broods a year, with young birds emerging as late as September.

Greenfinch (male and female) on dock

BULLFINCH

At 6 inches (15cm) in length quite a 'chunky' bird, with a black head, black and grey upper parts and a white rump and wing bars. The male has a deep crimson underside while the female's is a dull salmon-pink. Its beak is short and stubby, its diet berries, seeds and buds - the latter causing it to be very unpopular with fruit growers. Its song is a low piping warble, its call a soft 'peu-peu'.

Its nest is made of fine twigs, moss and lichen lined with rootlets and forming a platform or a cup in the branches of a shrub or tree. 4 or 5 eggs are laid: pale greenish-blue with dark, purplish-brown spots and streaks. There may be two or three broods a year.

Although a very attractive bird, its habit of eating the flower-buds of fruiting shrubs and trees has made it unpopular with gardeners and fruit-growers. (It was once even legal to shoot bullfinches, though they are now on the conservation list.) Where there are plenty of flowering shrubs and trees in the hedgerows it is less likely to attack orchards and gardens. It is also very fond of ash seeds (or 'keys'), which hang on the tree into spring, and will prefer to consume these.

Bullfinch (male) on blackthorn

CHAFFINCH

One of our commonest birds; it is 6 inches (15cm) long, the female is an overall olive-brown with white wing bars and outer tail feathers; the male has, in addition, a slate-blue crown, chestnut back, a greenish rump, and rufous underparts. Its song, given from an exposed perch, varies according to region but is basically a descending scale of notes, accelerating and ending in a flourish; its call is a ringing 'pick' and its flight call a short 'juep, juep'.

It often feeds on the ground from fallen weed seeds (or fallen crumbs in a tea garden!) but it also eats insects. The latter gives it the edge over some other finches as it is able to feed its nestlings with caterpillars, thus adding to the success of its breeding.

It nests in hedgerows, building a neat cup of grass, moss and lichens, lined with hair and containing 4-5 bluish or browny-white eggs, sometimes spotted. Breeding pairs of chaffinches are not sociable but later in the year are often seen in large flocks.

Chaffinch (male and female) with weed seeds

BUNTINGS

Compact, large-headed birds, with short, thick bills. They like open country with bushes and usually feed on the ground and nest in low bushes or on the ground.

YELLOWHAMMER

Quite like a big finch at 6½ inches (16.5cm) with a similar thick bill. The male is easily recognised by the bright yellow colouring on its head and underparts. The female's plumage is more subdued, browner and more streaked. Its rump is a chestnut brown, its wings and back are brown with black streaks, and it has white outer tail feathers. Its song, lustily sung from an exposed perch, is a rhythmic 'chic-iz-iz-iz-iz-iz-zee' or, as it's popularly known, 'a little bit of bread and no - cheese'. Its call is a sharp 'tjip'.

It likes open country with the cover of bushes or hedgerows. It generally feeds from seeds on the ground and, outside the breeding season, is often seen in flocks.

The female builds the nest in thick cover on the ground or a few feet up in a bush. The nest is a cup of grasses, plant stems and moss, lined with grass and hair. 3 or 4 eggs are laid, white or pale purplish with bold 'scribblings' on them.

Yellowhammer on pussy willow

SPARROWS

Small, thick-billed, short-legged birds. Gregarious - they breed in small colonies, feed on the ground and nest in holes or bulky domed nests. Their calls are unmusical chirps.

HOUSE SPARROW

A very common bird, closely associated with human habitation, though recently on the decline, possibly due to modern houses not providing suitable nesting places, such as eaves. It is 6 inches (15cm) long with streaked brown upperparts and paler beneath. The male has a grey crown and black bib. It has a familiar chirping song/call.

It will build a domed nest of straw and feathers in hedges and ivy-clad trees as well as in holes or under roofs. The nest contains 3-5 eggs and there may be two or three broods a year. The eggs are greyish-white with dark grey and greyish-brown speckles.

House sparrows enjoy taking dust baths in groups in summer and will splash in any water they can find. They will mingle with other finches in search of food - especially seeds - and in August will raid the farmers' fields of ripe grain.

House sparrow (male and female) with bramble

ACCENTORS

Small grey and brown birds with thin bills, of retiring habit. They are ground feeders.

DUNNOCK

Also known as a hedge-sparrow, though it is not a sparrow.

It is 5½ inches (14cm) in length with a stripy, brown back and a grey head and breast. It has a thin bill and feeds on the ground, searching for insects amongst scrubby vegetation, often beneath hedges. It will also feed on fruits in autumn. It is a common bird but often not noticed, or mistaken for a sparrow.

It has a high-pitched warbling song, of about two seconds at an even pitch, usually given from an exposed perch. The call is a piping 'tseep'.

The nest is cup-shaped, built in a bush or hedge, made from plant stems, fine twigs and roots, leaves and moss. The female lays between 3 and 6 bright blue eggs. There may be 2 or 3 broods a year.

Cuckoos often choose dunnocks' nests in which to lay their eggs.

Dunnock on dog rose

TITS

(the name 'tit' comes from 'titter' meaning anything small, or 'titchy'!)

Small, acrobatic birds, often quite tame and readily attracted to bird-feeders in the garden. They have short bills and will feed mostly on insects, seeds and nuts. Males and females are similar in colouring. They are often seen in mixed flocks; most nest in tree cavities.

BLUE TIT

One of the most common and familiar of the birds visiting our gardens, the blue tit is really a woodland bird, where it feeds in the tops of trees (including uncut hedgerows), rarely coming to the ground. Small, at 4 ½ inches (11cm) it is very acrobatic and colourful. It has a blue cap and bluish wings with white bars. Its upper parts are a greyish blue-green and the underparts a bright yellow. It has a black 'collar' and black 'spectacles' on a white face.

It has a trilling song and a varied call - often a repeated high-pitched 'zee'; sometimes both are combined.

It lines its nest hole, usually in a tree, with moss, dried grass, wool and dead leaves, and finally hair and feathers or down. The female will lay 7-10 eggs. The hatching of the nestlings in spring coincides with a glut of caterpillars - their main food. (A single large oak will harbour about 100,000 larvae of various insects.)

GREAT TIT

Bigger than the blue tit at 5 ½ inches (14cm) and with bolder markings. It has a black head and bib and white cheeks. The upper parts are bluish grey/green and underparts yellow. Its song is varied, though usually a characteristic series of penetrating 'zee-de' notes. Its call is a repeated 'pee-too'.

It is less gregarious than the blue tit, searching for food in low bushes, sometimes on the ground, but can be a bit of a bully to its smaller relatives, especially on a bird feeder.

Its diet is eclectic: buds, fruit, seeds, spiders and general household scraps. The nest is a cup of moss and grass lined with hair and down, in a tree or wall hole, containing 5-12 eggs. The nestlings are fed mainly on newly-hatched caterpillars.

Blue tit and Great tit on hazel

COAL TIT

The same size as the blue tit at 4½ inches (11cm) but less colourful. It has a black head with white on the cheek and nape of neck, and a buff/white underside. Its song is a repeated 'weetse' and its call a thin 'tset'.

Although it prefers coniferous woods it is common in deciduous or mixed woods and, outside the breeding season, in hedgerows. In the garden it tends to be dominated by the blue and great tits, and compensates for this by storing its food to ensure a supply over several days. It eats insects, seeds and bird table scraps.

It nests in a hole in a tree, tree stump, wall or bank, making a cup-shaped nest of moss lined with hair and feathers, containing 7-9 eggs.

MARSH TIT

Again 4 ½ inches (11cm) in length, the marsh tit is less commonly seen in the garden (where it is bullied by the more aggressive blue and great tits), preferring its natural habitats of deciduous woods and undergrowth (rarely marshes!).

It has a black cap and short black bib, white/buff undersides and brown upper parts. Its song is varied, sometimes a repeated 'tschuppi' and its call a scolding 'chickabeebee-bee-bee' or 'pitchu'.

The nest is a cup of moss in a tree or wall-hole, lined with hair and feathers, containing 5-9 eggs, timed to hatch when the caterpillars are most abundant.

Coal tit and Marsh tit on oak

Long-tailed Tit

Not a true member of the tit family but similar in its acrobatic skills and body-size - its tail is more than half its length, bringing it to 5½ inches (14cm). It is easily distinguished from the other tits by the length of its tail and its colouration. Its plumage is patterned black, white and pink on the upper parts, with a long black tail edged with white and white underparts tinged with pink.

It is invariably seen in small family flocks 'dancing' from tree to tree or along the hedgerow, never staying long in one place; its undulating flight accompanied by a high-pitched, thin 'see-see-see' call.

Unlike most birds, long-tailed tits roost in a huddle for warmth; they are particularly vulnerable to cold and many die in severe weather. This is compensated for, in terms of breeding success, by their family co-operation (unusual for birds). Much of their life is spent in family groups, they defend a group territory and even help at the nest of siblings if their own nesting attempts fail.

The nest is an oval shape, intricately made with moss bound together with cobwebs and hair and lined with feathers (as many as 2,000!) then camouflaged with an outer coating of lichen. It has a small entrance on one side and, once inside the nest, the birds have to fold their tails back over their heads to fit in. It is built in a tree fork or in thick shrubs or brambles and contains 8-12 white eggs.

Long-tailed tits on hawthorn

WRENS

Small, restless, brownish birds with rounded, often upturned tails, finely barred.

WREN

Our only member of the wren family, and one of our commonest birds. It is 4 inches (10cm) long with a characteristic short, rounded, upturned tail. Its plumage is all brown but prettily marked with bars on its tail. Its fine, sharp beak is used to catch insects. It has one of the loudest voices of all our small birds, with a piercing song made up of clear, high notes and trills; and a harsh grating call.

It seeks cover in thick foliage but can be glimpsed on short flights, fast, direct and low, between hedges or ivy-covered walls or tree trunks, where it also builds its nest (though it sometimes chooses more bizarre sites, often in sheds). The nest is ball-shaped with a high, side entrance, and made of dried grass, leaves and moss. The male constructs several shells of nests, the female chooses one (and him!) and lines it with feathers before laying 5 to 8 white eggs, speckled with black or reddish brown. Being a tiny bird it is very vulnerable to freezing winters and, though otherwise unsociable, is one of the few birds that roosts in a group for warmth on very cold nights (a record of 61 birds has been observed in one nesting box).

The males are very territorial and will defend their territories vociferously through autumn and winter.

Wren on ivy

Conclusion

There are of course many other birds to be seen on a hedgerow walk. From spring to autumn swallows skim low over the fields and hedges, grabbing insects in flight, along with the house martins and high-flying swifts. In autumn starlings will sometimes descend en masse on a fruiting shrub. The plump, comfortable wood pigeon will also feed on ripe berries.

Then there are the predators: the raptors - including buzzards, kestrels and sparrow hawks; the night-hunting owls and the ever-present crow family.

The existence of the hedgerow may be of secondary importance to these birds but they too play a vital role in its ecology.

10 TIPS FOR IDENTIFYING BIRDS

1. size
2. shape: stocky, long or short-tailed etc
3. shape of bill: thick, thin, long etc. indicative of diet
4. posture: more or less upright and/or agile
5. movements: darting, tail-flicking, acrobatic etc
6. flight pattern: straight, undulating, high or low etc
7. colour & patterning: (females often, juveniles always, less colourful)
8. song and call: rhythm, pitch, repetition etc
9. habitat (including nest site): scrub, bushes, trees etc
10. habits (including feeding): shy, bold, sociable - in flocks etc.

About the Author

Sandra has been painting plants and their associated invertebrates in watercolour since 1999 and has exhibited her paintings locally and in 'The Artist's Garden' exhibition at Rosemoor Royal Horticultural Society Gardens in Torrington. She sells her paintings regularly.

Prior to this she practised as a Medical Herbalist for nine years, during which time she published two booklets independently: *Growing Health* and *Wild Health*.

Before becoming a herbalist she was a schoolteacher in London for twenty three years and also taught part-time at Theobalds Park Environmental Study Centre for children. She studied Horticulture and Countryside Care and Conservation at Capel Manor in Hertfordshire, attended several Field Studies courses on wild flowers and the environment in Somerset and Devon and has herself given workshops, walks and talks on wildflowers and herbs. She has undertaken several photographic surveys, for her own interest, on wildflowers and herbs.

After moving to Devon with her husband in 1991 she became increasingly interested in the diverse wildlife of the area and of its hedgerows in particular. She keeps records for the B.T.O. (British Trust for Ornithology) - Garden Birdwatch, The Nunnery, Thetford, Norfolk IP24 2PU. (www.bto.org.uk)

SPECIES LIST

		Page
WARBLERS	Willow warbler on pussy willow	4
	Chiffchaff on elder	6
	Blackcap (male and female) on elder	8
	Garden warbler on bramble	10
	Whitethroat (male and female) on hawthorn	12
	Goldcrest (male and female) on ivy	14
THRUSHES	Robin on holly	16
	Blackbird (male) on rowan	18
	Song thrush with snail	20
	Mistle thrush, Redwing and Fieldfare	22
FINCHES	Goldfinch on spear-thistle	24
	Greenfinch (male and female) on dock	26
	Bullfinch (male) on blackthorn	28
	Chaffinch (male and female) with weed seeds	30
BUNTING	Yellowhammer on pussy willow	32
SPARROWS	House sparrow (male and female) with bramble	34
ACCENTOR	Dunnock on dog rose	36
TITS	Blue tit and Great tit on hazel	38
	Coal tit and Marsh tit on oak	40
	Long-tailed tits on hawthorn	42
WREN	Wren on ivy	44